BUILDING BETTER
FRIENDSHIPS

A 4-week course to help junior highers build stronger friendships

by Steve and Annie Wamberg

Group
Loveland, Colorado

Group®

Building Better Friendships
Copyright © 1992 Group Publishing, Inc.

Credits
Edited by Michael Warden
Cover designed by Jill Nordbye and DeWain Stoll
Interior designed by Judy Bienick and Jan Aufdemberge
Illustrations by Raymond Medici
Cover photo by David Priest

ISBN 1-55945-138-6
13 12 11 10 9 8 7 6 5   04 03 02 01 00 99 98 97
Printed in the United States of America.

CONTENTS

96926

BUILDING BETTER FRIENDSHPS

The door slammed. Three-thirty. It was Amy.

"Here comes the storm," Amy's mother sighed to herself.

"That Rachel!" yelled Amy as she thundered into the room. "She says she promised to go to Ellen's Friday, so she can't spend the night here! And we're supposed to be best friends!"

"Honey, calm down. Did Rachel say she isn't your friend, anymore?"

"No, but I was counting on her!"

● ● ●

"Man, it doesn't get any better than this. The stars, a campfire . . ."

"You sound like a beer commercial."

Jay and Denny laughed together. Jay smirked and said, "Gosh, Denny, you really know how to make a guy feel special."

"That's what friends are for. So are you really thinking about asking Kristi to the dance, or what?"

● ● ●

Remember the friends you had in your early teenage years? It probably seemed like several came and went as often as acne. Others might still be a part of your life today.

Friends are a critical part of adolescence, because peer relationships figure so heavily in the self-esteem of a teenager. Sadly, the normal roller coaster course of growing up sometimes makes junior highers become not-so-stable friends themselves, even as they search for— and demand—consistency in their own friends.

● 75 percent of Christian teenagers want to know how to make friends and be a friend

● 47 percent of Christian teenagers rarely or never talk to best friends about faith or God

● Only 13 percent of Christian kids report that their 3 to 5 best friends are "very religious"

Friends are confidants for teenagers. In a recent survey, friends topped the list of confidants used by both teenage boys and girls.

Friends are valued highly, and as adolescence continues, recognition of their value grows. Strong friendships have been listed as an important life value for three out of four high school seniors in surveys spanning two decades.

Biblical handles on what makes a good friend, and how to be one, can reassure junior highers that friends are worth pursuing, and that they themselves are worth having as friends. Also, considering Jesus as a friend can be greatly comforting to anyone.

This course offers biblical teaching and examples, including that of Jesus, to help junior highers discover just what makes good friendships "tick."

By the end of this course, your students will:
- discover the elements of a good friendship;
- gain greater understanding of how to handle conflicts in friendships;
- consider if they are truly being friends to others;
- review the risks and benefits of having a best friend; and
- consider how Jesus' sacrifice makes him an ultimate friend to them.

COURSE OBJECTIVES

HOW TO USE THIS COURSE

ACTIVE LEARNING

Think back on an important lesson you've learned in life. Did you learn it from reading about it? from hearing about it? from something you experienced? Chances are, the most important lessons you've learned came from something you've experienced. That's what active learning is—learning by doing. And active learning is a key element in Group's Active Bible Curriculum™.

Active learning leads students in doing things that help them understand important principles, messages and ideas. It's a discovery process that helps kids internalize what they learn.

Each lesson section in Group's Active Bible Curriculum plays an important part in active learning:

The **Opener** involves kids in the topic in fun and unusual ways.

The **Action and Reflection** includes an experience designed to evoke specific feelings in the students. This section also processes those feelings through "How did you feel?" questions and applies the message to situations kids face.

The **Bible Application** actively connects the topic with the Bible. It helps kids see how the Bible is relevant to the situations they face.

The **Commitment** helps students internalize the Bible's message and commit to making changes in their lives.

The **Closing** funnels the lesson's message into a time of creative reflection and prayer.

When you put all the sections together, you get a lesson that's fun to teach. And kids get messages they'll remember.

BEFORE THE 4-WEEK SESSION

● Read the Introduction, the Course Objectives and This Course at a Glance.

● Decide how you'll publicize the course using the clip art on the Publicity Page (p. 9). Prepare fliers, newsletter articles and posters as needed.

● Look at the Bonus Ideas (p. 45) and decide which ones you'll use.

● Read the opening statements, Objectives and Bible Basis for the lesson. The Bible Basis shows how specific passages relate to junior highers and middle schoolers today.

● Choose which Opener and Closing options to use. Each is appropriate for a different kind of group.

● Gather necessary supplies from This Lesson at a Glance.

● Read each section of the lesson. Adjust where necessary for your class size and meeting room.

BEFORE EACH LESSON

● The approximate minutes listed give you an idea of how long each activity will take. Each lesson is designed to take 35 to 60 minutes. Shorten or lengthen activities as needed to fit your group.

● If you see you're going to have extra time, do an activity or two from the "If You Still Have Time . . . " box or from the Bonus Ideas (p. 45).

● Dive into the activities with the kids. Don't be a spectator. The lesson will be more successful and rewarding to both you and your students.

● Though some kids may at first think certain activities are "silly," they'll enjoy them, and they'll remember the messages from these activities long after the lesson is over. As one Active Bible Curriculum user has said, "I can ask the kids questions about a lesson I did three weeks ago and they actually remember what I taught!" And that's the whole idea of teaching . . . isn't it?

Have fun with the activities you lead. Remember, it is Jesus who encourages us to become "like little children." Besides, how often do your kids get *permission* to express their child-like qualities?

HELPFUL HINTS

● The answers given after discussion questions are responses your students *might* give. They aren't the only answers or the "right" answers. If needed, use them to spark discussion. Kids won't always say what you wish they'd say. That's why some of the responses given are negative or controversial. If someone responds negatively, don't be shocked. Accept the person, and use the opportunity to explore other angles of the issue.

THIS COURSE AT A GLANCE

Before you dive into the lessons, familiarize yourself with each lesson aim. Then read the scripture passages.

● Study them as a background to the lessons.

● Use them as a basis for your personal devotions.

● Think about how they relate to kids' circumstances today.

LESSON 1: WHAT MAKES A FRIEND?

Lesson Aim: To help junior highers discover the elements of a good friendship.

Bible Basis: Proverbs 17:17; Matthew 11:18-19; and John 15:13.

LESSON 2: WHEN FRIENDS DISAGREE

Lesson Aim: To help junior highers know how to respond to conflicts in friendships.

Bible Basis: Proverbs 27:6; Matthew 5:23-24; and Matthew 18:15-20.

LESSON 3: BEST FRIENDS

Lesson Aim: To help junior highers examine the benefits and risks of having a best friend.

Bible Basis: 1 Samuel 20:1-42.

LESSON 4: THE ULTIMATE FRIENDSHIP

Lesson Aim: To help junior highers recognize the friendship qualities they can apply to their relationships with Jesus.

Bible Basis: Proverbs 18:24 and John 15:13-15.

PUBLICITY PAGE

Grab your junior highers' attention! Photocopy this page, and then cut out and paste the clip art of your choice in your church bulletin or newsletter to advertise this course on building better friendships. Or photocopy and use the ready-made flier as a bulletin insert. Permission to photocopy this clip art is granted for local church use.

Splash the clip art on posters, fliers or even postcards! Just add the vital details: the date and time the course begins and where you'll meet.

It's that simple.

Building Better Friendships

A 4-week junior high and middle school course on what it means to be a friend

Come to _____

On _____

At _____

Come learn how to build great friendships—and keep them going strong!

WHAT MAKES A FRIEND?

Just about any survey of kids' needs and wants will tell you how important friends are to teenagers. Even so, many kids don't really know what to look for in a friend. By helping junior highers recognize the qualities friends should have, we can help them build strong, healthy relationships.

LESSON AIM

To help junior highers discover the elements of a good friendship.

OBJECTIVES

Students will:
- consider what character traits and actions combine to make a good friend;
- create their own ideal friend;
- examine biblical guidelines of true friendship;
- analyze their own attitudes and actions as a friend to others; and
- commit to being a better friend.

BIBLE BASIS

PROVERBS 17:17
MATTHEW 11:18-19
JOHN 15:13

Look up the following scriptures. Then read the background paragraphs to see how the passages relate to your junior highers and middle schoolers.

Proverbs 17:17 describes the qualities of a true friend.

Solomon wrote much of Proverbs as a collection of "bits" of wisdom he'd picked up over the years. This particular verse gives us a picture of a real friend, one who's always available, and one who loves you—no matter what.

The search for friends who will accept them as they are is the quest of all junior highers. Like Solomon, kids need to learn what a real friend is like, so they not only can find true friendship, but also offer it to others.

Matthew 11:18-19 speaks of the people's perceptions of Jesus and John the Baptist during their ministries on earth.

In this passage Jesus confronted the people for basing their opinions of others on the company they keep. Jesus wasn't afraid to be friends with the less popular people of his day, no matter what others might have said about him.

Junior highers tend to be insecure about what others think of them—so much so that they'll often walk away from potentially good friendships for the sake of looking "cool." Kids need to see that Jesus spent time with the "uncool," yet never lost his own sense of personal value. Kids need to see they can do the same.

In **John 15:13**, Jesus describes the ultimate act of friendship.

During the last Passover meal before Jesus' death, Jesus spoke about love and told his disciples the ultimate sign of love and friendship is to die for a friend.

Junior high is a time of deep, changing feelings. Moods can shift from passion to trauma in the span of a few seconds. For kids to grasp the truth that real friendship means choosing to serve others over themselves opens the door for kids to gain a whole new depth of friendship—a friendship that sees love as an action, not just a feeling.

THIS LESSON AT A GLANCE

Section	Minutes	What Students Will Do	Supplies
Opener (Option 1)	5 to 10	**Friendship Factors**—Brainstorm qualities that make someone a good friend.	Paper, pencils, newsprint, marker, tape
(Option 2)		**Act Like a Friend**—Pantomime friendly actions.	
Action and Reflection	10 to 15	**Feats of Clay**—Sculpt the perfect friend.	Five colors of modeling clay
Bible Application	10 to 15	**Quality Check**—Consider biblical advice as they rate their own friendship qualities.	Bibles, "Quality Check" handouts (p. 17), pencils
Commitment	5 to 10	**Name That Quality**—Choose one friendship quality to improve on this week.	Construction paper slips, pencils, pins
Closing (Option 1)	5 to 10	**Friendship Collage**—Create a collage that illustrates friendship.	Old magazines, several rolls of tape, newsprint
(Option 2)		**Friendsing**—Sing along with a song about friendship.	Song about friendship, tape player

The Lesson

☐ OPTION 1: FRIENDSHIP FACTORS

Form groups of three or four. Give each group a piece of paper and a pencil. Instruct groups to come up with as many character traits or actions as possible that build good friendships. Allow them only a minute or two to work. Have groups compare lists and create a composite list on newsprint. Tape the composite list to the wall.

Say: **Most of us are willing to admit that we have friends! However, maybe we've never taken the time to analyze what makes our friendships work. This week we're going to look at friendship and see just how much we really know about it.**

☐ OPTION 2: ACT LIKE A FRIEND

Say: **Have you ever thought about what makes a good friend? What things do they do that show they are good friends? What qualities do they have?**

Instruct your class to not answer out loud, but to keep a mental list of their ideas. Have students each pick one of their ideas and take turns pantomiming it for the rest of the class to guess. Each person's idea must be original.

After each student has had a turn, say: **Phew! When you're trying to be a good friend, you don't realize how much there is to do! Today we're going to take a look at just what's involved in being a good friend.**

FEATS OF CLAY

Say: **We've come up with a lot of qualities important in a good friend, but which is most important? If you could pick only five qualities for your good friend, what would they be? You now each get the chance to be "Dr. Frankenfriend" and create the perfect friend!**

Give kids each five different colors of modeling clay. (If you don't have clay, you can use different-color construction paper instead.) Have kids work together to choose the five most important qualities of a good friend. When the list is complete, assign each quality to a particular color of clay.

Say: **I want you to sculpt the perfect friend, using each color of clay to the degree you want that quality in your friend. For example, if honesty is very important to you, and we've assigned the red clay to represent that quality, then you would sculpt a friend made up of mostly red clay.**

Allow kids about three minutes to sculpt their friend. When

OPENER
(5 to 10 minutes)

ACTION AND REFLECTION
(10 to 15 minutes)

everyone is finished, have kids each explain their sculptures. Then ask:

● **How did it feel to create your own perfect friend? Explain.** (It was fun, because it helped me to see what I really want in a friend; it was frustrating, because I don't think I'll ever find a friend like the one I created.)

● **How close is your "ideal friend" to what you're like with your friends? Explain.** (Close, but I'm not that loyal; not very close, I think I have different friendship qualities.)

● **How is your ideal friend like your friends in real life?** (Real friends aren't always so consistent; even my friends have qualities that bother me.)

● **Do you think a person can really be like your ideal? Why or why not?** (Yes, if someone really thought about it and worked at being a good friend; no, it's tough to let only good qualities show in your friendships.)

● **What could you do to become more like your ideal friend?** (I could try to be more understanding when my friends have problems; I could stop cutting down my friends so much.)

Say: **We've all heard the phrase, "You've got to be a friend to get a friend." That's really true. As we each work at becoming the kind of friend we want for ourselves, we'll find new friends with those qualities we're looking for.**

We have several great ideas of what a good friend is like. Now let's take a look at friendship from God's perspective.

BIBLE APPLICATION
(10 to 15 minutes)

QUALITY CHECK

Ask for volunteers to read aloud Proverbs 17:17, Matthew 11:18-19, and John 15:13. Ask:

● **What qualities do these verses say are important in a good friend?** (Friends stick by you; they help you when you're in trouble; they're friends even if others don't like you; they put your feelings before their feelings; they lay themselves down for you.)

● **How do these qualities compare with the qualities you felt were important?** (They're the same ones we had on our list; they're similar to mine; I think our list is better.)

● **How do you compare with the qualities listed in these verses?** (I have a long way to go before I'm that good of a friend; I think I do what those verses say most of the time.)

Pass out photocopies of the "Quality Check" handout (p. 17) and pencils. Give kids each a few minutes to rate themselves on how they'd react to the situations on the handout. When kids are finished, form pairs. Have partners tell each other about one real-life situation where a friend responded to them in a way that was really loving.

Read aloud the verses again. Then have kids each tell their partners one way that person is the kind of friend these verses describe.

Say: **All of us have some of the qualities that make for**

super friendships, but there's always ways we can each become more like the kind of friends God wants us to be.

NAME THAT QUALITY

Say: **Think about the different qualities we talked about today and about what the Bible thinks are important qualities of a good friend. Also, think about how you rated yourself on the handout. Based on all these things, pick one friendship quality you'd like to improve on this week.**

Pass out a slip of construction paper, a pencil and a pin to each person. Have kids each write the quality they wish to improve this week on their slip and pin it on their clothes. Group kids together according to the quality they've chosen. It's okay if all the qualities represented in one group aren't exactly alike. Just try to get similar qualities grouped together.

Have each group form a circle. Tell students each to pray for the person on their right, asking God to help him or her commit to be more (the chosen quality) this week. Encourage kids to tape their slips of paper to their notebooks this week as a reminder to work at developing that friendship quality.

Table Talk

The Table Talk activity in this course helps junior highers and middle schoolers talk with their parents about building healthy friendships.

If you choose to use the Table Talk activity, this is a good time to show students the "Table Talk" handout (p. 18). Ask them to spend time with their parents completing it.

Before kids leave, give them each the "Table Talk" handout to take home, or tell them you'll be sending it to their parents.

Or use the Table Talk idea found in the Bonus Ideas (p. 46) for a meeting based on the handout.

☐ OPTION 1: FRIENDSHIP COLLAGE

Set out a few stacks of old magazines where the kids can get to them. Tape a sheet of newsprint to the wall. Set out several rolls of tape.

Say: **One quality good friends have is that they can work together to accomplish a task. On "go" you'll all have four minutes to go through these magazines to find all the words and pictures you can to tell us everything there is to know about good friends. Oh, yes. In that four minutes you must not only find them, you must also arrange them in some wonderful way on this sheet of newsprint. Go!**

Call "time" when four minutes is up, and have volunteers explain different elements on the collage. Ask:

● **Is there anything about good friends that you didn't include on your collage? If so, what?** (Answers will vary.)

● **In what way is our collage like us as friends?** (We need each other to make a complete picture; as friends, we aren't complete yet either, just like our collage.)

Say: **Friends are important; we do need each other. Lets try to be conscious this week of just what kind of friend we should be to the people around us.**

Close with prayer, asking God to help kids be good friends this week.

☐ OPTION 2: FRIENDSING

Before class, obtain a copy of a song about friendship, such as "Friends," "Lean on Me" or "You've Got a Friend." Form a circle and play the song for kids. Have them sing along.

After the song, ask:

● **How true is this song to real life?** (Answers will vary depending on which song you play.)

● **Is it possible to build friendships with the qualities this song describes? Why or why not?** (Maybe, if my friends are willing to work at it, too; I'm not sure, it seems like it would take more commitment than most people are willing to give.)

Say: **Songs can tend to make anything sound easy. We know that friendships take time and work. But we also know that we have what it takes to be good friends. Let's pray together and ask God to help us be the best friends we possibly can be.**

Close with sentence prayers.

If You Still Have Time . . .

Circle of Friends—Have the kids take the clay "friends" they built and connect them in a circle on a table where they can remain throughout the course on friends. Have kids each write out the quality composition of their clay friend and put that list under their figure. Have kids compare the different strengths of their clay figures and talk about how they can be sensitive to each person's unique needs in friendship.

Friendship Builders—Have the kids refer to the qualities they wrote on their construction paper slips. Have kids brainstorm practical ideas they might use this week to develop those qualities. Encourage them to come up with many ideas so kids with different levels of courage will have good ideas to use in the coming week.

✔ Quality Check

Rate yourself! How do you think you'd react to these situations? Read each entry and put a check in the column that best describes how closely your reaction would be to what's written. Be honest!

Allie had hurt Meg's feelings badly, but wanted to make things right. She approached Meg at school the day after their fight and said she was sorry. Meg responded, "That's nice, but I'm just not ready to forgive you." Would you respond like Meg?

I'd respond like Meg:

Always   Sometimes   Never!

Ned knew Gregory from church. He didn't mind hanging out with Gregory at church, but at school, Gregory was, well, a lot different than the other kids. One day Gregory caught sight of Ned in the hall and tried to give him the "Jesus Jab" handshake they'd made up at church. Ned ignored him and walked on. Would you have done the same?

I'd respond like Ned:

Always   Sometimes   Never!

Sarah and Kyle had grown up next door to each other, but they'd gone in different directions as they grew older. The night Sarah's dad died, Kyle sat up with her and her family even though it meant he'd miss the team bus to the basketball final. Would you make the same choice?

I'd respond like Kyle:

Always   Sometimes   Never!

Table Talk

To the Parent: We're involved in a junior high course at church called *Building Better Friendships*. Students are exploring a Christian perspective on friendship. We'd like you and your teenager to spend some time discussing this important topic. Use this "Table Talk" page to help you do that.

Parent

Respond to the following questions:
- Who was your best friend in junior high?
- What was he or she like?
- Why do you think you were best friends?
- Where is that friend now?
- Do you still have any friends from your junior high years?
- If so, why do you think those friendships have lasted? If not, why not?

Junior higher

Respond to the following questions:
- Who is your best friend?
- What do you look for in a best friend?
- Have you ever thought of your parent(s) as a friend(s)? Why or why not?
- In what ways is your parent(s) like a friend(s) to you? In what ways is your parent different?
- In what ways are you like a friend to your parent(s)?
- How could your parent(s) be a better friend to you?
- How could you be a better friend to your parent(s)?

Parent and junior higher

Respond to the following questions:
- How is God like a best friend?
- How can you become a best friend to God?
- How can you help each other become a better friend to God? to each other? to others?

As a family, brainstorm two or three creative projects you can do together to build friendships with each other and with God. Do one project each week for the next two or three weeks.

WHEN FRIENDS DISAGREE

"Conflict" has become a dirty word in our society. Because of unresolved conflict, at least half of the marriages in our country end in divorce. Kids learn the lie early on—that conflict inevitably destroys relationships. Therefore, conflict should be avoided at all cost.

But conflict doesn't have to be bad. When kids learn how to deal effectively with conflicts in their relationships, it can actually become the soil that allows relationships to grow deeper.

To help junior highers know how to respond to conflicts in friendships.

Students will:
- **consider why conflicts in friendships happen;**
- **experience the frustration of conflict;**
- **discover biblical principles about friendship and conflict; and**
- **develop strategies to work through conflicts to make a friendship stronger.**

Look up the following scriptures. Then read the background paragraphs to see how the passages relate to your junior highers and middle schoolers.

Proverbs 27:6 says that wounds from a friend can be trusted.

This proverb was written by a man who most likely knew what it meant to receive empty flattery. As king, Solomon depended on those close to him to be honest with him. He wanted them to tell him the truth about himself and his

LESSON AIM

OBJECTIVES

BIBLE BASIS
PROVERBS 27:6
MATTHEW 5:23-24
MATTHEW 18:15-20

leadership—even if their words might be painful.

Junior highers need to learn the difference between criticism and correction. When they see that criticism is based on judgment, while correction is based on love, then they can learn not only to give correction from a loving heart, but also to receive it.

Matthew 5:23-24 talks about resolving conflicts with others before we come before God.

Jesus taught that it's important to resolve conflicts. God doesn't want strife between two people, so he directs us to resolve our conflicts before we come to worship him.

It seems characteristic of humans to avoid conflict and to nurture grudges. But kids can learn to deal quickly and directly with conflict, so their relationships with each other and with God remain healthy.

Matthew 18:15-20 gives guidelines to resolving conflicts when someone has sinned against you.

Jesus taught that dealing directly with conflict is the best way to handle it. He tells us to go immediately to someone if you feel you've been wronged by that person. Instead of publicizing the wrong, Jesus here offers steps to heal the relationship as quietly as possible.

The gossip grapevine is a popular form of communication among junior highers as well as adults. By following Jesus' instructions in this passage, kids can learn to redeem their broken relationships rather than destroy them.

THIS LESSON AT A GLANCE

Section	Minutes	What Students Will Do	Supplies
Opener (Option 1)	5 to 10	**Disagree-ercise**—Experience disagreement with others.	
(Option 2)		**Decorate a Disagreement**—Illustrate words that describe feelings when they disagree.	Paper, pencils, markers, crayons
Action and Reflection	10 to 15	**Communication Breakdown!**—Experience disagreement due to improper communications.	"Communication Breakdown" handouts (p. 26), paper
Bible Application	10 to 15	**When the Bubble Burst**—Discuss personal examples of conflict in friendship in light of biblical principles.	Slips of paper, balloons, pencils, Bibles
Commitment	5 to 10	**Agree to Disagree**—Analyze their own tendencies when facing conflicts in a friendship.	"Agree to Disagree?" handouts (p. 27), pencils
Closing (Option 1)	5 to 10	**Decorate a Disagreement Revisited**—Illustrate words that describe feelings when they know conflict will improve a friendship.	Paper, pencils
(Option 2)		**Dear Friends . . .**—Write a letter to a friend that describes how they'll handle conflict in their friendship.	Paper, pencils

The Lesson

☐ OPTION 1: DISAGREE-ERCISE

Form pairs and send one person from each pair out of the room. Instruct the remaining kids to disagree with whatever their partners say or do when they return. Tell them they don't have to be mean about it—just disagreeable.

Bring the partners back in. Tell pairs you're going to give them a quick list of tasks to perform. Let kids know they will have to work quickly. When you call out a new assignment, pairs must abandon what they're working on and go on to the new one. Give them only half a minute or so per assignment.

Take the class through a series of quick directions. Say: **You're getting a new animal. First, decide what kind of animal you're getting.** *(Pause for half a minute)* **Second, decide what to name it.** *(Pause)* **Third, work up a schedule of who feeds and gives any other care to the animal.** *(Pause)* **Fourth, decide where the animal will sleep.** *(Pause)*

Is everything decided between you? No? There's a reason for that! Your partner was instructed to disagree with you about everything you would discuss.

Ask:

● **How did you feel when your partner disagreed with all your ideas?** (Like I was being ganged up on; frustrated.)

● **The things I gave you to decide weren't too tough. Still, why is it sometimes hard for people to agree on things like that?** (They both think they have the best idea; they don't trust the other person.)

● **How were the conflicts and feelings you felt similar to what happens between friends sometimes?** (Sometimes the little things are the hardest to agree on; I get angry when my friends disagree with me, just like I did in this activity.)

Say: **Conflict is almost never fun, but it's essential to a healthy relationship. Today we're going to talk about the right and wrong ways to handle conflict.**

☐ OPTION 2: DECORATE A DISAGREEMENT

Give each person a sheet of paper and a pencil. Instruct kids each to write on their paper one word that describes how they feel when they disagree with a friend. Then have them decorate the word to make it "look" like the feeling the word represents. For example, if the word is "hurt," they could draw spikes coming out of the word.

Say: **It's not very pleasant when friends disagree, but disagreements are inevitable. Everyone faces them. Let's take a closer look at how we should deal with conflicts in relationships.**

ACTION AND REFLECTION

(10 to 15 minutes)

COMMUNICATION BREAKDOWN!

Form pairs. Pass out one set of "Communication Break-down" slips (p. 26) to each pair. Warn kids not to look at their partner's slip, or anyone else's. Give a sheet of paper to each pair with two slips.

Say: **Read your slip, and then put it in your pocket. You may not see what the other person has on his or her slip. You both have the same basic task to accomplish. You have a limited time in which to do your task.**

Give your class about three minutes to accomplish the tasks. Then ask:

● **How many of you were able to get your tasks done?** (Answers will vary.)

● **What would have helped you get your task done more effectively?** (If we'd been able to talk about the things we were supposed to do; if I could have seen the other slip.)

● **How did you feel during the exercise?** (Frustrated; like my partner wasn't trying to work with me.)

● **How do you think this activity is like conflict in real life?** (We all want to do things our own way, even when friends disagree; we get worked up over unimportant things.)

● **What kind of strategy did you use to get your task done?** (We didn't get done; we took turns doing the task each other's way.)

● **How could that same strategy, or a strategy like it, be applied to real life situations where friends disagree?** (Sometimes when you think you're disagreeing you're just coming at the same thing from different angles; we really need to listen to each other more.)

● **What do you think causes real life friends to have disagreements?** (Lack of communication; wanting to do things differently; assuming the other agrees with you all the time; not asking how the other feels about stuff.)

● **How can we avoid those things we just mentioned?** (Don't assume your friend always wants to do the same thing you do; keep checking with your friends to see what they're feeling and thinking about things.)

Say: **Try as we might, sometimes things just go wrong between friends. Let's check out what the Bible says about working things out when friends disagree.**

WHEN THE BUBBLE BURST

Give a slip of paper, a balloon and a pencil to each student. Depending on the size of your class, you may wish to have the kids work in pairs or small groups. On their slip, have kids each write a two-sentence description of a disagreement they had with a friend, including what it was about and what caused it. Then have kids each roll up their slip, put it in a balloon, inflate it and tie it off. Put all the balloons in a pile and allow each student (or group) to choose one balloon that isn't the one they placed in the pile. When everyone has a balloon, have kids each pop their balloon and come up with a way to resolve the conflict described on the paper.

After all the kids have offered their solution, ask:

● **How did you feel about helping solve someone else's problems?** (Good; I felt nervous about giving bad advice.)

● **How different was it from solving your own problems?** (I felt a lot more levelheaded about someone else's problem than I do about mine; the answer seemed obvious.)

● **Do you think the answers you gave could really work in real life? Why or why not?** (Probably, if both sides agree to do it; maybe not, my answer doesn't seem practical.)

● **Can disagreements between friends ever be good? If so, when?** (Sometimes yes, when a disagreement keeps a friend from getting into trouble; yes, if a disagreement can help you understand the other person better.)

Say: **The conflicts we talked about are from real life, and we came up with some interesting ways to resolve them. But how many of our solutions do you think were solutions God would choose? God has set up ways for us to resolve conflicts. Let's see how close our ideas were to what the Bible suggests we do.**

Have volunteers read aloud Proverbs 27:6; Matthew 5:23-24; and Matthew 18:15-20. Then ask:

● **The verse in Proverbs seems to say that there are times when friends actually do us a favor by hurting us. Can you think of an example?** (Any time a friend says or does something to keep me from hurting myself; if a friend stops me from doing something that really offends her.)

● **How would you sum up Jesus' advice in Matthew 5:23-24?** (Take care of disagreements as quickly as you can; don't pretend that everything's all right if it isn't.)

● **Why do you think it's so important to work quickly to resolve conflicts with your friends?** (The longer you wait, the more it hurts your friendship; if you wait, you could start developing a grudge.)

● **Why do you suppose that Jesus taught in Matthew 18:15-20 to first go directly to someone with whom you have a problem?** (So you won't talk about that person behind his back; so you won't get other people to not like that person.)

● **Based on these passages, what happens when friends**

actually resolve their differences? (You can stay friends; you can learn from each other.)

● **What do you feel is the toughest thing about resolving conflicts with friends?** (Saying I'm sorry; facing the fact that we might never agree about some things.)

● **How do you feel about Jesus' teaching about conflicts in friendships?** (It's hard but possible; I don't think I could do it.)

Say: **Whenever we have a conflict, it's natural to want to withdraw from the person we're arguing with. But Jesus teaches us that nobody wins when we don't try to resolve our conflicts with others. It takes courage. But more than that, it takes love.**

AGREE TO DISAGREE

Distribute photocopies of the "Agree to Disagree?" handouts (p. 27) and pencils. Give kids a few minutes to rate themselves. Encourage kids to go with their first response. Have kids compare their answers with each other. Then ask:

● **In one word, how would you describe your feelings when you disagree with a friend?** (Uncomfortable; frustrated; unsure of myself; angry; hurt.)

● **How would you like your friends to act toward you when they disagree with you?** (I'd still like them to act like my friend; I want them to be honest with me.)

● **Think of the last time you disagreed with a friend. How could you have changed the way you acted to make things go more smoothly?** (I could've been calmer; I guess I could've not been so mean.)

Have students gather in a circle and say to the person to their right, "Even when we disagree, you're a friend worth keeping." Then have volunteers go around the circle and tell each person one thing that makes him or her a "friend worth keeping."

Say: **Conflicts are actually good for a friendship; they serve to bring the people closer together. Let's commit together this week to take the disagreements that might come up and allow them to make us better friends.**

Have kids pray silently, committing to God that they'll work at resolving their conflicts with friends this week.

☐ OPTION 1: DECORATE A DISAGREEMENT REVISITED

Give kids a sheet of paper and a pencil. Have them each put one word on the page that describes how they feel when they have a conflict with a friend, but they know the friendship will improve because of it. Have them decorate the word to show the word's meaning. For example, if the word is "hope," someone might draw a sunrise or an unopened present. Have kids each explain their drawing to the rest of the class.

COMMITMENT
(5 to 10 minutes)

CLOSING
(5 to 10 minutes)

Close with prayer, asking God's help in dealing with conflicts his way.

☐ OPTION 2: DEAR FRIENDS ...

Give each student a sheet of paper and a pencil. Have each person write a letter to a real friend that completes these thoughts:

Dear_____,

If we ever have a disagreement, I will try to never _____
_____. I will try to
_____.

Have kids each sign their letter. Lead junior highers in a prayer of commitment to try to be the kind of friends they wrote about in their letters. Encourage them to apply God's ways of resolving problems this week.

If You Still Have Time ...

Face to Face—Form two groups. Have the groups face each other. Have one group come up with a conflict between friends, and then have the other group come up with a solution of how to handle that conflict. Then reverse roles.

Disagreement Cheers—As a class or in smaller groups, have kids create cheers that talk about how people can disagree and still be friends. Have the class perform their cheers, then give themselves a round of applause.

Communication Breakdown

Make enough copies of these instructions to give each pair in your group one set.

1a. You and your partner must pick one shoe that ties. Your task is to untie and retie the shoe.

1b. You and your partner must pick one shoe that ties. Your task is to untie, unlace, relace and retie the shoe.

2a. You and your partner may have one sheet of paper. Your task is to fold the paper into four square sections.

2b. You and your partner may have one sheet of paper. Your task is to fold the paper into four triangular sections.

3a. You and your partner must walk around the room arm in arm. You must go around clockwise, on your knees.

3b. You and your partner must walk around the room arm in arm. You must go around counter clockwise, hopping.

AGREE to DISAGREE ?

Read the following situations. Rate the situations on a scale of 1 to 10 (1 = zero influence exerted; 10 = megatons of influence exerted), based on the amount of influence you'd try to exert to get your friend to change his or her behavior.

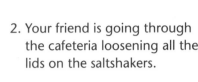

1. Your friend wants to go to a party where you know there will be drugs.

   1   2   3   4   5   6   7   8   9   10

2. Your friend is going through the cafeteria loosening all the lids on the saltshakers.

   1   2   3   4   5   6   7   8   9   10

3. Your friend meets you before school wearing the ultimate gross-out-of-the-year outfit.

   1   2   3   4   5   6   7   8   9   10

4. You notice your friend reading information from a group that you think is a cult.

   1   2   3   4   5   6   7   8   9   10

5. Your friend is involved in spreading a false rumor about someone nobody in school really likes.

   1   2   3   4   5   6   7   8   9   10

6. You notice that every day after lunch your friend goes to the bathroom to throw up.

   1   2   3   4   5   6   7   8   9   10

7. You happen to be around when your friend steals money from his parents.

   1   2   3   4   5   6   7   8   9   10

8. Your friend likes heavy metal, while you like dance music.

   1   2   3   4   5   6   7   8   9   10

LESSON 3

BEST FRIENDS

For junior high kids, "best friends" can seem to come and go as quickly as the rain in spring. Today Marcia is Kate's best friend, but tomorrow it could be Sarah or Yolanda. In such volatile times, junior highers can benefit from understanding why best friends are so important to them and what it really takes to have one.

LESSON AIM

To help junior highers examine the benefits and risks of having a best friend.

OBJECTIVES

Students will:
● discuss what factors separate best friends from other friends;
● perform a reader's theater based on David and Jonathan's friendship;
● talk about the pros and cons of having best friends; and
● develop ways to strengthen the relationships with their best friends.

BIBLE BASIS
1 SAMUEL 20:1-42

Look up the following scriptures. Then read the background paragraphs to see how the passages relate to your junior highers and middle schoolers.

First Samuel 20:1-42 tells the story of David and Jonathan's friendship against the backdrop of King Saul's treachery.

When David and Jonathan met, they struck up an almost instant friendship. But Saul's jealousy of David was so great that Saul tried to kill David. Jonathan had to choose between his father's wishes and his love for David. He made his choice. Jonathan stayed true to David, and protected him from Saul, even though the cost was high.

David and Jonathan were best friends. But that means more than just having good times together. Sometimes friendships bring costs. Junior highers can benefit from knowing that being someone's best friend carries with it the advantage or disadvantage of others associating you with that person. It's wonderful to have a close friend, but there are risks involved, too.

THIS LESSON AT A GLANCE

Section	Minutes	What Students Will Do	Supplies
Opener (Option 1)	5 to 10	**"Across" Friendship**—Create an acrostic that describes best friends.	Paper, pencils
(Option 2)		**Best Reflection**—Tell about the first best friends they ever had.	
Action and Reflection	10 to 15	**You're My Best Friend**—Experience the favored status or the exclusion felt when some, but not all, have best friends.	Cookies, decorating icing
Bible Application	10 to 15	**You're On!**—Perform a reader's theater of David and Jonathan's friendship.	Bibles, newsprint, marker, tape, "The Sally Oprah-Rivera Show" handouts (pp. 34-35)
Commitment	5 to 10	**The Best Friendships**—Discuss lists of advantages and disadvantages of best friend relationships.	Newsprint, markers, masking tape, pens
Closing (Option 1)	5 to 10	**Talk About Your Friend**—Make a three-item prayer list to pray for one of their best friends this week.	Paper, pencils
(Option 2)		**Best Friends Best Fun**—Talk about fun times they've had with best friends.	

The Lesson

☐ OPTION 1: "ACROSS" FRIENDSHIP

Say: **We all have ideas in our head about how to define friendship, but the real test is putting those thoughts into words that really explain what we mean to other people. Now you get your chance.**

Form pairs, and give each pair a sheet of paper and a pencil. Have each pair do an acrostic of the words "best friend." Have pairs explain their acrostic. Then say: **Best friends can be great! We may all want to be someone's best friend, but today we may find that being a best friend costs more than we think.**

OPENER
(5 to 10 minutes)

☐ OPTION 2: BEST REFLECTION

Form a circle. Go around the circle and have students each tell who their first best friend was, how they met and when they were friends. If kids say they've never had a best friend, have them tell about a good friend.

Ask:

● **What made that person your best friend?** (Same interests; lived near me; the only person my age on the block.)

Say: **There's something very special about your first best friend, even if that friendship is part of your past. This week we're going to look closely at the many sides of being best friends.**

YOU'RE MY BEST FRIEND

Have kids form a line, and send every third person into the hall or off to a side room. Pair off the rest of the kids. Tell the pairs they are now best friends. Give the best friends two cookies and a tube of decorating icing. Tell the pairs to decorate their cookies and enjoy them together while you invite the remaining kids to return. Give no other instructions.

When the remaining kids return, have each stand next to a pair of best friends, and tell them to stay quiet and watch. After all the cookies are eaten, call everyone together and ask:

● **How did you feel about having a best friend just now?** (I felt like I was somebody special; I felt uncomfortable, because we're really not that close.)

● **How did those of you who had best friends feel toward those who came in later?** (I felt sorry for them; I felt like they didn't belong.)

● **If you didn't have a best friend, how did it feel to be around them?** (I felt really out of place; I felt like they didn't like me.)

● **Did any best friends share their cookies with someone who came in later? Why or why not?** (Yes, we really thought they needed to feel included; no way, you didn't tell us we had to.)

● **Do you think having best friends makes others feel left out? Why or why not?** (Yes, others might feel left out, because you focus so much on your best friend; no, because having a best friend doesn't mean you can't have other friends, too.)

● **What are the advantages of having a best friend?** (You have someone special to count on; you know someone else is watching out for you.)

Say: **Best friends can be a great asset. Sometimes they can be costly, too. Let's take a look at scripture to find out the pros and cons of having a best friend.**

ACTION AND REFLECTION

(10 to 15 minutes)

YOU'RE ON!

Form three groups, and assign each group one of these passages: 1 Samuel 20:1-17; 1 Samuel 20:18-34; and 1 Samuel 20:35-42. Give groups each newsprint and a marker, and have group members work together to summarize each passage in three sentences. Have them write their sentences on the newsprint, then tape the newsprint to the wall.

After reading the summaries aloud, ask:

● **In your own words, how would you describe the relationship between David and Jonathan?** (Jonathan loved David more than his father; they were really close.)

● **How would you describe the relationship between David and Saul?** (They didn't like each other; Saul was out to get David.)

● **How did Jonathan and David's friendship affect Saul?** (It made Saul angry; it made Jonathan a traitor in Saul's eyes.)

Pass out photocopies of the sketch, "The Sally Oprah-Rivera Show," (pp. 34-35) to your class. Assign the parts. Have all the kids who don't have parts act as the live audience. After kids perform the sketch, ask:

● **In the sketch, David and Jonathan talked about the advantages of being best friends. But from what you could tell from the Bible passages for today and the sketch, what are some possible risks in having or being a best friend?** (Someone might get really jealous of the relationship; you might ignore other people who are also important in your life.)

● **What are the qualities in David and Jonathan's relationship that made them best friends?** (They were loyal to each other; they watched out for each other; they took risks for each other that they might not have taken for just anyone.)

● **One important aspect of David and Jonathan's relationship was that they shared the same belief in God. What would you advise a Christian to do if their best friend isn't a Christian?** (Really let your friend see you be faithful to God in your actions and words; find another best friend.)

● **Honesty is important in any relationship. When do you think it might've been hard for David and Jonathan to be honest with each other?** (When David had to tell Jonathan that Saul was trying to kill him; when Jonathan had to let David know that David would have to go away.)

● **What might have happened if they hadn't been honest?** (David might have died; Jonathan could've betrayed David by telling Saul where he was.)

● **Based on this passage, what kind of person does it take to be a best friend?** (You have to be totally honest and loyal to your friend; you have to put your friend's need above your own.)

Say: **Now that we've explored David and Jonathan's friendship, let's take a few minutes to discuss what we think about best friendships.**

COMMITMENT
(5 to 10 minutes)

THE BEST FRIENDSHIPS

Form two groups. Provide each group with newsprint and markers. Have one group make a list of as many advantages of being or having best friends as they can. Instruct the other group to list disadvantages of best friendships. Give each group a chance to read its list to the other group.

Ask:

● **Is having a best friend worth it? Why or why not?** (Yes, because it's so important to have someone who you know is always on your side; no, it takes too much effort to keep it going.)

● **Whether we have best friends or not, how can today's material help us make all of our friendships stronger?** (We can work at staying loyal to all our friends; I can spend more time with other people besides my best friend.)

● **What's one thing you'll do this week to make your close or best friendships better for everyone?** (I'll ask someone else to go along with me and my best friend; I'll tell my close friend I'd like to be best friends with her.)

Give a strip of masking tape and a pen to each person. Tell them to stick the tape onto their shoulders. Say: **Best friends stick together, even when times are hard. Each of us has what it takes to be a best friend, if we choose to. Turn to the person on your right and write on their tape one quality that person has that would make him or her a great best friend.**

CLOSING
(5 to 10 minutes)

☐ OPTION 1: TALK ABOUT YOUR FRIEND

Give each student a sheet of paper and a pencil. Instruct them to come up with a prayer list of three things to pray for their best friend this week. (If they don't have one particular best friend, just have them pick one friend to pray for this week.) Have them begin their prayer time for their best friend with a few moments of silent prayer before class is over.

Close with prayer, thanking God for best friends and asking him to help kids be the best friends they can.

☐ OPTION 2: BEST FRIENDS, BEST FUN

Go around the room, allowing the kids to take turns telling about the most fun time they've had with their best friend (or a good friend). After everyone has had a turn, vote on which story wins the "Most Fun Time" award, the "You Had To Be There" award and the "Most Bizarre Fun" award.

Close with prayer, thanking God for close friendships and asking for guidance to make all our friendships strong.

If You Still Have Time . . .

Friendship Scramble—Form two teams. Write the word "friendship" in big letters on newsprint or a chalkboard. Have teams separately list all the words they can come up with that use the letters in the word "friendship." The only rule is that the words must relate in some way to the topic of friendship.

Thank You Notes—Give kids each a 3×5 card and a pencil, and have them each write a thank you card to their best friend (or a close friend)—just to thank them for their friendship. Encourage kids to give their cards to their friends this week.

THE SALLY OPRAH-RIVERA SHOW

CAST

Sally Oprah-Rivera   David
Jonathan   Saul
Audience Members   Announcer

ANNOUNCER: Welcome to the Sally Oprah-Rivera Show! Here's your host—Sally Oprah-Rivera! *(Enthusiastic applause)*

SALLY: Thank you, thank you. Well, you've read the story by now in First Samuel 20. Some people call it a scandal. Some people don't know what to think. But whatever *you* think, I think it's a hot topic for discussion. Today's topic: "When a Father Really Doesn't Like His Son's Best Friend." Let's welcome our guests now—King Saul, Jonathan and David! *(Enthusiastic applause)*

SALLY: Okay guys, now why do you think your relationship has become so intense?

DAVID: Sally, excuse me for interrupting, but it's all my fault.

SAUL: You said that right!

SALLY: We have an audience member ready to follow up on my original question.

AUDIENCE MEMBER 1: Saul, your highness, why do you have such hard feelings toward David?

SAUL: I could write a book about it! Let's just put it this way. I go fight wars; everyone thinks David is a hero. I try to organize a government; everyone wants David to lead them. I try to raise a son; *(looks at Jonathan and glares)* he prefers David to me.

JONATHAN: Dad, it's not the same.

AUDIENCE MEMBER 2: I'd like to ask a question.

SALLY: Okay, go ahead.

AUDIENCE MEMBER 2: Yes, another question for his highness, Saul. Sir, it sounds to me like you'd probably be jealous of David whether or not he was your son's best friend. Am I right?

SAUL: Uh . . . ahhh . . .

JONATHAN: Yes, I think he'd be jealous, anyway.

SAUL: But hey! Things are bad enough with David without you having him for a friend. I'm trying hard to keep our family in the palace . . .

DAVID: By killing me?

JONATHAN: By killing him? Dad, I couldn't believe my ears when David told me that you wanted him dead. I had to check out his story.

SAUL: So you plotted against me!

DAVID: All he did was try to keep me safe, Your Highness.

SAUL: Like I said, he plotted against me!

AUDIENCE MEMBER 3: Jonathan, here's my question: Even though you're a prince and would take over your dad's throne when he dies, you stuck up for David? I mean, David's the one Samuel anointed to be king after your father!

SAUL: Listen to this, son, it makes sense!

AUDIENCE MEMBER 3: Do you understand that if David survives, you lose your chance at the throne—maybe forever?

JONATHAN: I know. But aren't friends worth more than being a king? *(Enthusiastic audience applause)*

SAUL: That's exactly the kind of drivel I'm talking about. Jonathan, you never talked like that before this—this David came into your life!

JONATHAN: Of course not. I never had a friend so great before I met David. It was like our souls were knit together right from the start.

SALLY: David, do you have anything to say? You're being awfully quiet.

DAVID: Well, it's really hard for me. *(Pause)* See, I love and respect the king. *(Audience gasps and murmurs)*

AUDIENCE MEMBER 4: But he's trying to kill you!

DAVID: I know. *(Pause)* How do I explain? The King is God's anointed. He's still my king . . .

SALLY: That's pretty loyal talk for a guy who has a price on his head.

JONATHAN: That's one of the things that make him such a good friend. Dad, you ought to be ashamed of yourself! How can you hate a guy like this?

SAUL: *(Exploding)* You only listen to what you want to hear! I am the <u>king</u>! If I say someone should die, then he must die! The king has spoken! This friendship can lead to no good. You are my son! I am the King! David must die!

SALLY: We're just about out of time for today's show. One last question for both David and Jonathan: What makes you two best friends?

JONATHAN: You don't always plan on best friends, Sally. Sometimes things just click between two people and a deep friendship develops. Beyond that, David has proven trustworthy and loyal to me. How many other people would stick around to be my friend after my dad has thrown a spear at him?

SALLY: Good point! And you, David?

DAVID: Jonathan is nobility, born and raised in a palace. I'm a shepherd and grew up with a bunch of stinky sheep and my harp. But Jonathan has never let the difference in our stations make any difference in our friendship. That's a true friend.

SALLY: I, for one, think it's refreshing to see two young men who are committed to friendship as deeply as you two are. Thank you for being on my show today. And thank you, King Saul, for agreeing to be here as well. *(Applause)*

LESSON 4

THE ULTIMATE FRIENDSHIP

For junior highers, friendships are usually their number one priority. And the importance of friendships only grows as kids go on to high school. Because of this, adolescence is a great time to show kids how Jesus can be their best friend! No friend can be perfect—except Jesus. And he's waiting for kids to come to him even now.

LESSON AIM

To help junior highers recognize the friendship qualities they can apply to their relationships with Jesus.

OBJECTIVES

Students will:
● consider what traits and actions would make up "the ultimate friend";
● recognize the need to have God for a friend;
● discuss how Jesus can become their best friend; and
● commit to apply the aspects of friendship to their relationship with Jesus.

BIBLE BASIS
PROVERBS 18:24
JOHN 15:13-15

Look up the following scriptures. Then read the background paragraphs to see how the passages relate to your junior highers and middle schoolers.

Proverbs 18:24 tells us that having lots of friends isn't as wonderful as a "friend who sticks closer than a brother."

Solomon knew that friendship goes deeper than shallow social contacts. The wisdom applied in this verse indicates that it is possible—and desirable—to have close friendships where those involved are relationally closer than some family members. That sort of friendship, Solomon notes, is rare.

Teenagers hunger for the rare friendships this passage describes. Proverbs 18:24 is often used today in direct reference to the kind of relationship we can have with Jesus Christ.

Teenagers need to be encouraged that the ultimate friendship for them rests with Jesus alone.

In **John 15:13-15**, Jesus tells his disciples that he looks at them as friends, not servants.

The disciples were human. Often, they didn't understand what Jesus was doing or teaching. They probably often wondered what Jesus thought of them. Jesus assured the disciples in these verses that they were his friends. Jesus defines the greatest love as laying down one's life for friends and describes friends of his as those who do what he commands.

Early adolescents learn by doing. They need to know what they need to do to be Jesus' friend. Jesus' words indicate that they need to do what he commands and imply that they need to establish a personal relationship with Jesus as his disciple. Kids should be encouraged to respond obediently as they think of Jesus as a friend and reflect on how Jesus' sacrifice showed his ultimate friendship for them.

THIS LESSON AT A GLANCE

Section	Minutes	What Students Will Do	Supplies
Opener (Option 1)	5 to 10	**Utopian Friend**—List qualities of the ideal friend.	Newsprint, markers
(Option 2)		**Cliffhangers**—Brainstorm cliffhangers and discuss how an ultimate best friend would solve them.	3×5 cards, pencils
Action and Reflection	10 to 15	**Putting It All Together**—Put puzzles together with one piece missing.	"24-Piece Puzzle" handouts (p. 42)
Bible Application	10 to 15	**Picture This**—Create a mural based on their biblical understanding of Jesus as a friend.	Bibles, tape, newsprint, markers, crayons
Commitment	5 to 10	**How Do You Treat a Friend?**—Complete handouts to apply positive friendship factors to their relationship with God.	"Friendship Treatment" handouts (p. 43), pencils
Closing (Option 1)	5 to 10	**Another Cliffhanger**—Discuss cliffhangers and how Jesus would resolve them.	3×5 cards from Cliffhangers Opener or 3×5 cards, pencils
(Option 2)		**Friendship Bracelets**—Weave a friendship bracelet with a Bible verse reference written on it.	Three shoelaces of equal length for each student, fine-point markers

The Lesson

☐ OPTION 1: UTOPIAN FRIEND

Have the class list on newsprint qualities of the ultimate best friend. No quality is too wild, even if they think it's impossible for someone to fulfill.

After the class has had a few minutes to develop the list, review it with them. Then ask:

● **Do you really know anyone that might fulfill all these positive qualities? Explain.** (No, no one's that perfect; yes, I have a really good friend who seems to fulfill the list.)

● **If you had that sort of friend, what would you want him or her to do for you as a friend?** (I'd want him to always be with me; I'd like her to show me how to be that kind of friend.)

Say: **It's nearly impossible to think of any human totally fulfilling the role of an ultimate friend. Before you give up hope, though, think about this—what about God as a friend? Maybe Jesus could fulfill these qualities for you and be an ultimate friend. We'll look at that possibility this week.**

☐ OPTION 2: CLIFFHANGERS

Have the class sit in a circle. Give a 3×5 card and a pencil to each student. Have kids each write a cliffhanger—a really tough situation that looks impossible to get out of—about anything on their card, and then pass the card to the person on their left. That person must write how the ultimate friend might rescue the person or resolve the problem, and then pass the card to the person on their left. Have that person read the card to the rest of the class.

After one round of Cliffhangers, ask:

● **In real life, can your friends do everything the ultimate friends can do? Why or why not?** (No, nobody's that consistent and perfect; no, they'd have to be Superman.)

● **When you're in trouble, who do you tell first—your friends or God? Explain.** (I tell my friends, because it's not always easy to talk to God; I tell God everything.)

Say: **There are friends you go to school with and friends you think of calling immediately when you're in trouble. Have you ever thought of God as your friend? We'll look at that possibility in this week's lesson.**

PUTTING IT ALL TOGETHER

Form seven groups. A group can be one person. Give six of the groups each a cut apart photocopy of the "24-Piece Puzzle" handout (p. 42). Give the seventh group a different piece from each of the puzzles (so there is only one piece missing from each puzzle). Tell the seventh group to watch the others struggle to put together the puzzles, which can only be completed with their help. Allow the groups with puzzles to reach a point of frustration.

After several minutes, allow the seventh group to go around and help the other groups complete their puzzles. Ask:

● **How did you feel when you couldn't do your puzzle on your own?** (Frustrated; cheated.)

Ask the seventh group:

● **How did you feel while you were watching the other groups try to finish their puzzle on their own?** (Like I was in on a secret; like I was in control; I wanted them to hurry so I could fix it for them.)

Ask:

● **Once you found out where to go for the missing piece, how did you feel asking someone else for help?** (It was no big deal; it was frustrating, because I felt like we were set up.)

● **How did those of you holding the missing pieces feel when the other groups were asking you for help?** (Like I had a lot of power; needed.)

● **How would those of you with the missing pieces feel if you knew the others wouldn't come to you for help, even though they needed you?** (Frustrated; like they were being stupid.)

● **Which of these two types of groups is most like God? Explain.** (The group with the missing pieces, because God brings us what's missing in our lives; the missing piece group, because God's always willing to help us out.)

● **Do you think that God can be a friend to you, like the seventh group was? Why or why not?** (Yes, but I wonder if God really notices me; yes, God always wants to be my friend.)

Say: **All through history God has been trying to tell us that he wants to have a relationship with each of us. Not just as a ruler or a judge, but as an intimate friend! Don't just take my word for it; let's look at what God says.**

PICTURE THIS

Read aloud Proverbs 18:24 and John 15:13-15. Ask:

● **How can a friend be closer than a brother?** (Some friends listen to you better than even family members; some friends stick with you in tough times, even when your family doesn't.)

● **How is God like the friend in Proverbs 18:24?** (God

always listens; God loves you; God is always there for you.)

● **How could you be a friend to God like the friend in Proverbs 18:24?** (I could work harder at listening to and obeying God; I could stick by what I know God wants, no matter what.)

Read aloud John 15:13-15 again. Ask:

● **What sort of things do you think people who want to be Jesus' friend will do, according to this passage?** (They'll do what Jesus wants them to; they'll take care of each other.)

● **How does Jesus show us he is our friend?** (He died for us; he wants us to be his friends, not just his servants.)

Tape a large sheet of newsprint to the wall. Make plenty of markers and crayons available to your class. Have kids create a mural to illustrate how Jesus is the ultimate friend. Encourage them to think both in terms of what Jesus did in New Testament times to prove his friendship and how his friendship affects their lives today. Try to allow enough time to let them feel as though they've produced a quality piece of work.

Say: **You did a wonderful job of illustrating Jesus' friendship. One big thing we can learn from Jesus' example is sacrifice. Friends sacrifice for each other. Jesus is the ultimate example of that, and that's why we can believe him when he says he's our friend.**

HOW DO YOU TREAT A FRIEND?

Pass out a photocopy of the "Friendship Treatment" handout (p. 43) to each student. Give each person a pencil. Allow a few minutes for kids to complete the handout, then have volunteers tell the class what they wrote for #3.

Say: **We all have solid ideas of what it takes to be a good friend and what a close friend God wants to be with each of us. All the things we can do to make our earthly friendships strong can be the same things we use to build a strong relationship with God.**

Lead the class in a prayer of commitment to treat God in the same positive ways they treat their other friends. After the prayer, form groups of three, and have kids each tell their group members one way they see Jesus' kind of friendship in each of the other members.

☐ OPTION 1: ANOTHER CLIFFHANGER

Gather the 3×5 cards the kids used in Cliffhangers Opener, and pass them out randomly to the class. (If you didn't use that Opener, just have kids create a fresh set of cliffhangers according to the instructions listed in the Opener.) Have kids each write a fresh resolution to their cliffhanger using Jesus as the ultimate friend coming to the rescue. Have kids explain their cliffhangers to the group.

Close with prayer, thanking God for sending Jesus to be our ultimate friend.

COMMITMENT
(5 to 10 minutes)

CLOSING
(5 to 10 minutes)

☐ OPTION 2: FRIENDSHIP BRACELETS

Pass out three shoelaces of equal length to each student (with one being white, if possible). With a permanent fine-point marker, have kids each write "John 15:13-15" on the white lace. Then instruct the kids to braid the three laces together.

Have the kids form pairs, and have them each tie the bracelet to their partner's wrist. After they have on their "ultimate friendship" bracelet, have kids form a circle and pray together, thanking God for his friendship and the friendship of those around them.

If You Still Have Time . . .

Still More Bracelets—Provide the students with more shoelaces to make friendship bracelets for someone outside the class. Encourage them to give the bracelet to someone who could really use the encouragement of knowing they have a friend.

Course Reflection—Form a circle. Ask students to reflect on the past four lessons. Have them take turns completing the following sentences:

- Something I learned in this course is . . .
- If I could tell my friends about this course, I'd say . . .
- Something I'll do differently because of this course is . . .

24-PIECE PUZZLE

FRIENDSHIP TREATMENT

1. List the three most positive things you do for your friends regularly:

2. List the three most positive things God has done for you:

3. Write one way you can apply your answers from #1 to your relationship with God:

BONUS IDEAS

Bonus Scriptures—The lessons focus on a select few scripture passages, but if you'd like to incorporate more Bible readings into the lessons, here are some suggestions:

● Leviticus 19:16-18 (God commands us to love our neighbors.)

● 2 Samuel 1:23-26 (David laments the deaths of Saul and Jonathan.)

● Proverbs 27:17 (The writer compares friendship to the sharpening of iron.)

● 1 Corinthians 13 (Paul talks about the supremacy of love.)

● 1 Corinthians 15:33 (Paul warns against choosing the wrong friends.)

● James 4:4 (James warns Christians to not be friends with the "world.")

A Friend to View—Compile a videotape of excerpts from several TV shows that show friends in conflict and coming through for each other. View them and discuss what makes good and bad friendships, how the situations could have been handled better and how it might have been different if Jesus was brought into the situations.

Diary of a Real Friendship—Have kids compile pictures, mementos and short write-ups of fun times with a close friend. Have students each put these together in a small album to give to their friend as a celebration of their friendship.

I Have the Most Friends—Form teams of four to six. Have each team come up with a list of songs, movies, TV shows, slogans, catch phrases, morals or proverbs, or Bible verses that talk about friends or friendship. When teams are ready, have them each read their list. Award points for each answer that does not match another team's. The team with the highest score wins.

Videofriend—Let kids create a video advertisement for a "friend for sale." Videotape the ads over a week's time, then show them during a regular meeting or at a retreat. Discuss why friends are so important and what it takes to be a good friend.

Everyone Says—Have kids create a list of survey questions to discover what people think about friendship. Get permission to go to a mall to give the survey. Take information from a

---

MEETINGS AND MORE

wide age-range. Have kids compile the information, then post the findings for the youth group and the rest of the church.

Secret Friend—At the beginning of the course, have kids each select a name of a class member out of a hat. That person becomes their "secret friend" for the duration of the course. Tell kids each to do one thing every week for their secret friend, such as send a card, give candy or plant "secret surprises" in their school locker or on the front porch of their home. Reveal the identities of the secret friends during the last week of the course, or at a retreat or party.

Your-My-Our Friend—As a class, pick a person from outside the class who needs a friend. Provide a list of suggestions to help kids along. For example, it could be a shut-in from your church or a young person who just moved to town. Do special things as a class for that person each month for at least three months.

Visual Words—Pass out a photocopy of the "Visual Words" handout (p. 48) and a pencil to each student. All of the "visual words" pictured have something to do with friends, and all of them use a form of the word "friend" in the answer. Form pairs, and have a contest to see which pair can finish first.

The answers are: 1. friendship; 2. friend in need; 3. fair-weather friend; 4. faithful friends; 5. friend to the end; 6. friends for life; 7. friend indeed; 8. a friend lays down his or her life; 9. friend or foe; 10. a friend sticks closer than a brother; 11. a friend loves at all times; and 12. a friend through thick and thin.

Table Talk—Use the "Table Talk" handout (p. 18) as the basis for a meeting with parents and junior highers. During the meeting, have parents and kids complete the handout and discuss it. Divide parents and kids into two separate groups, and have each group create a "friend" collage using newsprint, markers and other art supplies. On their collages, have groups identify the qualities that are needed to be a great friend. Have groups compare their collages, and discuss similarities and differences. Talk about how parents and junior highers can become better friends to each other at home.

PARTY PLEASER

BYO Friend—This is a "celebration of friendship" party. Kids may bring only a *friend* to the party—no dates.

Before the party, write on separate sheets of paper the following names of famous friends (one name per sheet): Wayne/Garth; Bush/Quayle; Sherlock Holmes/Dr. Watson;

Tarzan/Cheeta; Han Solo/Chewbacca; Lone Ranger/Tonto; Batman/Robin; David/Jonathan; Captain Kirk/Mr. Spock; Laverne/Shirley; Bill/Ted; King Arthur/Merlin; Lucy Ricardo/Ethyl Mertz. Fold each sheet in half to hide the name.

As the pairs arrive, pin or tape a set of famous friends to their backs without letting them see who they now are (pairs are on their honor to not peek at each other's back). When you're ready to start the activity, have pairs each show their new identity to the rest of the kids and ask three yes-or-no questions to figure out who they are. After one round, if neither partner can figure out who they are, allow a second round of questions. If the pair still can't figure it out, have the rest of the kids offer hints until the pair gets it.

Serve food that starts with an "f" for friendship. Allow kids to use only "f"orks (even if eating "f"rozen yogurt!) Give each pair of friends a chance to tell "f"unny stories on each other. Have pairs team up against other pairs in a series of fun "friend-olympic games," such as a three-legged race, or three-legged and three-armed Twister. Award prizes that begin with "f" for the winners in each activity.

RETREAT IDEA

A Friend in Need—Hold a daylong retreat that focuses on serving others as friends. Before the retreat, secretly get permission from the kids' parents to do the following "Samaritan" activity. At the beginning of the retreat, read the story of the Good Samaritan (Luke 10:25-37). Ask kids, "Who is my neighbor?" Have the kids agree to help out their neighbors in need. Load the kids up into cars and take them to their homes. Have kids each go through their closet and find three items of clothing to give to the needy. Be sure they choose only quality items.

Have all the cars meet at a designated time to go to a homeless shelter to offer their gifts of friendship. After the activity, return to the church to debrief. Play several crazy friendship games; eat a meal together; and close with prayer, thanking God for giving to us so we can give to others.

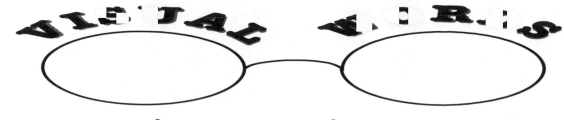

1.

2.

nefriended

3.
**sunny
buddy**

4.

5.
Amigo2finish

6.
BUDS
LIFE   LIFE
LIFE   LIFE

7.

DEFRIENDED

8.
COMPANION

9.

compadre
adversary

10.
pal   twigs

bro

11.
CLOCK

12.
T H R O U G H

T H R O U G H

Answers:

1. _____
2. _____
3. _____
4. _____
5. _____
6. _____
7. _____
8. _____
9. _____
10. _____
11. _____
12. _____